A BASKET OF BANGLES
HOW A BUSINESS BEGINS

GINGER HOWARD   ILLUSTRATED BY CHERYL KIRK NOLL

THE MILLBROOK PRESS
Brookfield, Connecticut

For
Lea Redmond
—G. H.

Acknowledgments
Many thanks to David Bornstein. This book would not have been
possible without the firsthand observations of the Grameen Bank in his book
The Price of a Dream. Thanks also to Rob Rooy, producer of the video
To Our Credit, which first brought micro-lending to my attention. And thanks to
Samir Hasan, field accountant with the Grameen Bank, for insightful changes and
colorful additions to the text. Lastly, and most importantly, sincere gratitude goes to
the working women who have shared their inspiring stories.
References: David Bornstein *The Price of a Dream: The Story of the Grameen Bank*,
New York: Simon & Schuster, 1996.
Rob Rooy, Rooy Media A Two-Part Video Series, 1998: *To Our Credit: Bootstrap
Banking and the World*, and *To Our Credit: Bootstrap Banking in America*; Rooy Media,
P.O. Box 2007, Frederick, MD 21705   www.toourcredit.org

Library of Congress Cataloging-in-Publication Data
Howard, Ginger.
A basket of bangles / Ginger Howard ; illustrated by Cheryl Kirk Noll. p. cm.
Summary: With seed money borrowed from a bank, a young woman and four of
her friends in Bangladesh change their lives by starting their own businesses.
ISBN 0-7613-1902-6 (lib. bdg.)
[1. Women—Employment—Fiction. 2. Entrepreneurship—Fiction. 3. Women—
Bangladesh—Fiction. 4. Bangladesh—Fiction.] I. Noll, Cheryl Kirk, ill. II. Title.
PZ7.H8284 Bas 2002   [Fic]—dc21   2001037071

Published by The Millbrook Press, Inc.
2 Old New Milford Road, Brookfield, CT 06804

Sufiya knew everyone in the village. Every day she walked from house to house begging for rice.

At night she slept on the floor of her brother's house.

"Why don't you start a business?" asked a villager one day.

"I have no money," Sufiya replied.

"Go to the bank meeting. They have money to loan."

On Wednesday, Sufiya went to the meeting at the center house.

"Yes, we have money to loan," said the manager.

"What business will I have? How will I earn money?" asked Sufiya.

"That is for you to decide. Come back when you have an idea. You also need four friends to borrow money with you."

Sufiya decided she would sell bangles. Then she looked for four friends to be in her borrowing group.

Khatun wanted to sell milk.

Aleya wanted to sell soap.

Peara wanted to sell snacks to the children at school.

Rokeya wanted to sell saris.

The next Wednesday the five ladies went to the center house. "We are ready for our loans."

"Can you write your names? Do you know the rules of the bank?" asked the manager.

"I can write my name," said Rokeya. But the other four could not.

"Each one must know how to write her name. And learn to say the rules."

The ladies left the center house. Rokeya showed her friends how to write their names. They practiced for two days.

Then the ladies went to visit Taslima. Taslima had borrowed money the year before to buy a sewing machine. "Will you teach us the rules of the bank?"

"Of course. Come in."

The five ladies recited the rules over and over:

"We will follow the four principles of the bank: Discipline, Unity, Courage, and Hard Work.

We will save a little money each week for emergencies.
We will repair our homes when they are damaged.
We will grow vegetables to feed our families.

We will drink water from the well, or we will boil our water.

We will build latrines.

We will send our children to school.

We will always be ready to help one another."

The next Wednesday the five ladies returned to the center house. They recited the rules. The bank manager gave Sufiya 2,000 taka. The bank would charge her 20% interest to borrow the money for one year. Sufiya signed her name on a paper promising to pay the money back. She would have to pay back 2,000 taka and 400 taka interest. She would pay the bank 40 taka each week for fifty weeks. On the fiftieth week, she would also pay 400 taka for interest.

The bank manager gave the other four ladies 2,000 taka each. They all signed their names on the loan papers.

"You must help one another," the bank manager said. "I want to see all of you here each Wednesday. If one of you is sick and cannot come to pay, then the rest of you must pay for her."

The next morning, the five ladies started their businesses. Sufiya, Khatun, Aleya, and Peara walked to the village bazaar. Rokeya rode the bus to the city.

Sufiya bought a large basket. She bought lots of brightly colored bangles. Since she was buying so many at once, the shopkeeper gave her a special price. Each bangle cost her 6 taka.

Khatun bought a cow.

Aleya bought a goat.

Peara also bought a large basket. Then she bought packages of muri and mango pickles.

Rokeya rode to the city on a crowded bus for three hours. She kept her face hidden behind her veil. At the market, she bought 6 finely woven saris.

Sufiya walked from house to house in the village as she had done many times before. But today her hands were not empty. "Would you like to buy a bangle?"

"They are beautiful! I'll take two, one for me and one for my daughter. How much are they?"

"Ten taka each."

Sufiya put the 20 taka in her sari. By the end of the day, Sufiya had sold 15 bangles. She had 150 taka in her pocket. The 15 bangles had cost only 90 taka. Sufiya had earned 60 taka.

Sufiya bought some rice and lentils and a cooking pot. That night she made dinner for herself and her brother. She cooked a little extra to eat in the morning. Then she put 8 taka in a box to save for the interest due on the fiftieth week. And she put 2 taka in another box to save for emergencies.

Khatun tied her cow to a tree. She milked the cow every day and sold the milk.

Aleya tied her goat to a bush. Every day she milked the goat. She boiled the milk, mixed it with oils and herbs, and poured it into soap forms. She sold the soap once a week at the bazaar.

Peara made a nice arrangement of muri and mango pickles in her new basket. She walked to the school and waited in the yard. The first day the children didn't have any money. They looked hungrily into the basket. The next day Peara was waiting again. She sold every package of muri and every mango pickle.

Rokeya walked from house to house to sell her saris. Once a week she took the bus to the city to buy more. The women of the village had never seen such finely woven cloth. They loved the shimmering colors.

Every Wednesday the five ladies walked to the center house. Sufiya paid 40 taka to the bank. Khatun, Aleya, Peara, and Rokeya did the same.

After a few months the five ladies had some extra money. Sufiya bought a sheet of tin to cover a hole in her brother's roof. Khatun bought a mosquito net for her bed. Aleya bought a kerosene lamp so her daughter could study at night. Peara bought a stone mortar and pestle so she could grind chili peppers into paste for curry. And Rokeya bought a petticoat—the first one she had ever owned!

One night there was a terrible thunderstorm. The streets filled with mud. Lightning crackled through the village.

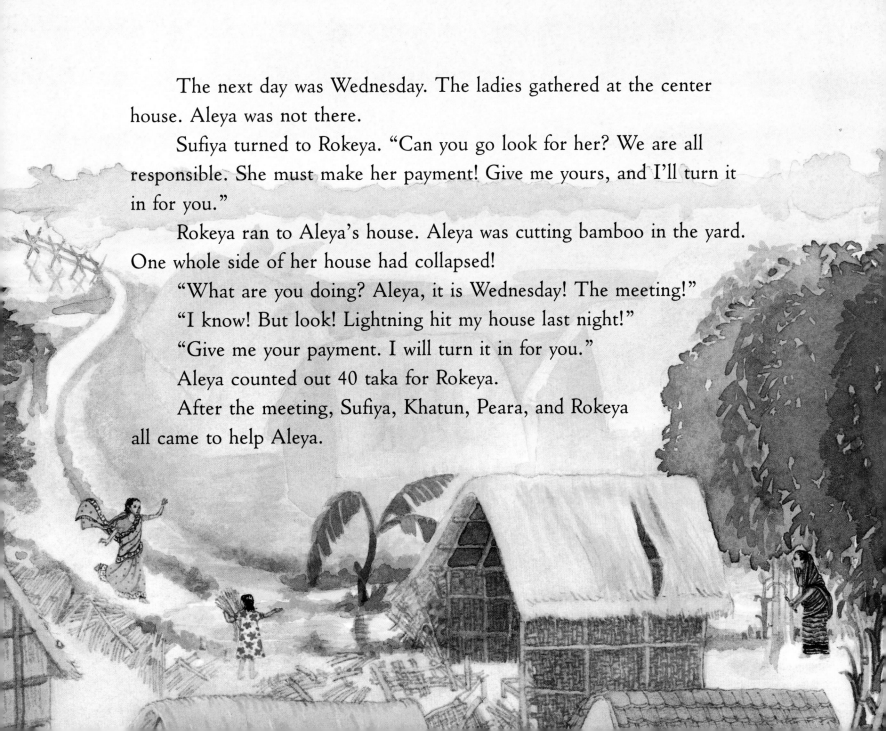

The next day was Wednesday. The ladies gathered at the center house. Aleya was not there.

Sufiya turned to Rokeya. "Can you go look for her? We are all responsible. She must make her payment! Give me yours, and I'll turn it in for you."

Rokeya ran to Aleya's house. Aleya was cutting bamboo in the yard. One whole side of her house had collapsed!

"What are you doing? Aleya, it is Wednesday! The meeting!"

"I know! But look! Lightning hit my house last night!"

"Give me your payment. I will turn it in for you."

Aleya counted out 40 taka for Rokeya.

After the meeting, Sufiya, Khatun, Peara, and Rokeya all came to help Aleya.

Finally it was the fiftieth Wednesday. Sufiya made her last payment of 40 taka. Then she paid 400 taka for the interest. The other four members of her group did the same. The loans were paid back, and the interest was paid.

"You are very trustworthy," said the manager. "We thank you for your business."

The ladies walked to Aleya's house to celebrate. She served rice, bean curry, and fresh goat's milk. Peara brought biscuits and molasses.

Sufiya said, "I can cook my own rice every day now. But I have another idea. I want to buy a little piece of land and grow my own rice. I could sell the extra in little packages with my bangles."

Khatun said, "I would like to buy another cow so I will have more milk to sell."

Aleya said, "My goat has two kids and I own them, too. I would like to buy some chickens and ducks. I could sell the eggs."

Peara said, "I want to buy my own cart. I could visit more schools and carry more snacks."

Rokeya said, "I would like to rent a stall at the bazaar to sell my saris. Then I could fill the shelves, and customers would have a greater selection."

The next Wednesday, the five ladies walked to the center house.
They recited the rules. They signed their names. And they walked out
with new loans tucked in their saris.

Is this story true?
The women in this book are not real people, but their stories could be true. There are thousands of women like Sufiya and her friends all around the world.

Why is Sufiya so poor?
Sufiya lives in Bangladesh, a country of frequent natural disasters. Cyclones, tidal waves, and floods often tear apart houses and ruin crops. In this story I imagined that Sufiya lost everything in a great flood. Her brother does not have extra money or food to give her.

What are muri and mango pickles?
Muri is puffed rice, similar to American breakfast cereal. A spicy muri might be made with onion, tomato, sweet potato, green chilies, and chili powder. A sweet muri might have peanuts and fresh coconut on top. Mango pickles are slices of dried mango mixed with spices and oil. The spices are often coriander, cumin, and mustard seeds, chopped onion and garlic, and chili powder.

What is a taka?
Just like the dollar in the United States, Bangladesh has the taka. Although 1 U.S. dollar is worth about 57 taka, 1 dollar and 57 taka do not buy the same things. The cost of living is different in Bangladesh than in the United States. In Bangladesh, a box of eight crayons costs 6 taka, a loaf of bread costs 12 taka, and a pair of sneakers costs about 250 taka.

Do all banks loan money like this?
No. Most banks would not help Sufiya and her friends. Most banks would require Sufiya to own something that is worth the amount of money she wants to borrow. Then, if Sufiya did not repay her loan, the bank could take her possessions in place of the payment.

Does the bank in this story really exist?

Yes! It is called the Grameen Bank and was started by Professor Muhammad Yunus in Bangladesh. He had the idea that a bank could loan money to groups of people, and they could help each other pay the loans back. There are more than one billion people in the world who earn less than one dollar per day. That is one-fifth of all the people in the world. Dr. Yunus says, "Credit should be accepted as a fundamental human right."

Can Sufiya and the bank both make a profit?

Sufiya wants to start a business and earn money. The bank needs to earn money, too. It works like this:

The bank gives Sufiya 2,000 taka (the loan) and charges her 400 taka for the service (the interest). Sufiya now owes the bank 2,400 taka. The bank will use part of the interest to pay the bank manager's salary.

Sufiya buys 240 bangles for 6 taka each. She spends 1,440 taka. She now has 240 bangles and she has 560 taka leftover.

Sufiya sells the bangles for 10 taka each and earns 2,400 taka, which she pays back to the bank.

Sufiya has 560 taka left. She can use this money to buy food, to save for emergencies, and to buy more bangles! As long as she can buy bangles for less than she sells them for, she will continue to earn a profit, and support herself.

Do you want to learn more about the Grameen Bank?

Write to:
Grameen Foundation USA
1709 New York Avenue NW, Suite 101
Washington, DC 20006
www.gfusa.org
www.peoplesfund.org

Taka